50 Premium Chinese Restaurant Dishes for Home

By: Kelly Johnson

Table of Contents

- Peking Duck
- Kung Pao Chicken
- Mapo Tofu
- Sweet and Sour Pork
- Mongolian Beef
- General Tso's Chicken
- Beef with Broccoli
- Sizzling Mongolian Lamb
- Cantonese Dim Sum
- Shrimp with Lobster Sauce
- Hot and Sour Soup
- Wonton Soup
- Egg Foo Young
- Honey Walnut Shrimp
- Braised Abalone with Shiitake Mushrooms
- Orange Chicken
- Char Siu (Chinese BBQ Pork)
- Salt and Pepper Shrimp
- Chicken with Cashew Nuts
- Dry-Fried Green Beans
- Lemon Chicken
- Shrimp and Scallop Stir-Fry
- Chinese Spicy Beef and Peppers
- Steamed Fish with Ginger and Scallions
- Kung Pao Shrimp
- Imperial Prawns
- Steamed Dumplings
- Pork and Chive Dumplings
- Chinese Broccoli with Oyster Sauce
- Sweet and Sour Chicken
- Twice-Cooked Pork
- Eggplant with Garlic Sauce
- Crispy Duck with Pancakes
- Chinese Chive and Shrimp Dumplings
- Sichuan-style Chicken
- Beijing-style Noodles

- Xiao Long Bao (Soup Dumplings)
- Lotus Root with Pork Soup
- Prawns in Black Bean Sauce
- Stir-Fried Lobster with Ginger and Scallions
- Shrimp Spring Rolls
- Scallops with Chinese Mushrooms
- Beef Chow Fun
- Shrimp Fried Rice
- Red-braised Pork Belly
- Cantonese Roast Chicken
- Fried Tofu with Vegetables
- Stir-fried Asparagus with Shrimp
- Crab Rangoon
- Hot Pot with Tofu and Vegetables

Peking Duck

Ingredients:

- 1 whole duck (about 5-6 lbs)
- 1 tbsp maltose syrup (or honey)
- 1 tbsp soy sauce
- 1 tbsp rice vinegar
- 1/2 tsp five-spice powder
- 2 tbsp hoisin sauce
- 12-16 Chinese pancakes (available at Asian markets)
- Cucumber, julienned
- Scallions, sliced thin

Instructions:

1. Preheat your oven to 350°F (175°C).
2. Rinse and pat dry the duck. Remove any excess fat and trim the neck.
3. In a small bowl, mix the maltose syrup, soy sauce, rice vinegar, and five-spice powder.
4. Brush the duck with the glaze mixture, ensuring it's fully covered.
5. Roast the duck for 1.5 to 2 hours, basting every 30 minutes.
6. Once the skin is crispy and golden, remove the duck from the oven.
7. Let the duck rest for 10 minutes before carving.
8. Serve with hoisin sauce, pancakes, cucumber, and scallions for wrapping.

Kung Pao Chicken

Ingredients:

- 1 lb chicken breast or thigh, cubed
- 1/4 cup soy sauce
- 1 tbsp rice vinegar
- 2 tbsp hoisin sauce
- 1 tsp sugar
- 1 tbsp cornstarch
- 2 tbsp vegetable oil
- 1/4 cup unsalted peanuts
- 3-4 dried red chilies
- 1/2 red bell pepper, chopped
- 1/2 green bell pepper, chopped
- 1/4 cup green onions, chopped
- 1 clove garlic, minced
- 1 tsp ginger, minced

Instructions:

1. In a bowl, mix the soy sauce, rice vinegar, hoisin sauce, sugar, and cornstarch to create a sauce.
2. Heat the oil in a wok over medium-high heat. Add the dried chilies and cook until fragrant.
3. Add the chicken cubes and stir-fry until golden brown and cooked through, about 5-6 minutes.
4. Add the garlic, ginger, and bell peppers, and stir-fry for 1-2 minutes.
5. Add the sauce and cook for another 2-3 minutes until the sauce thickens.
6. Stir in the peanuts and green onions.
7. Serve hot with steamed rice.

Mapo Tofu

Ingredients:

- 1 block firm tofu, cubed
- 1/2 lb ground pork (or beef)
- 2 tbsp soy sauce
- 1 tbsp doubanjiang (fermented chili paste)
- 1 tbsp rice wine
- 1 tbsp ginger, minced
- 2 cloves garlic, minced
- 1 tbsp Sichuan peppercorns
- 1/4 cup chicken stock
- 2 tbsp vegetable oil
- 2 green onions, chopped
- Cooked rice for serving

Instructions:

1. Heat the oil in a pan over medium-high heat. Add the Sichuan peppercorns and fry for 1-2 minutes until fragrant.
2. Add the ginger, garlic, and ground pork, cooking until the pork is browned.
3. Stir in the doubanjiang, soy sauce, and rice wine.
4. Add the chicken stock and bring to a simmer.
5. Gently add the cubed tofu to the pan and let it simmer for 5-7 minutes.
6. Garnish with green onions and serve with steamed rice.

Sweet and Sour Pork

Ingredients:

- 1 lb pork tenderloin, cut into bite-sized pieces
- 1/2 cup cornstarch
- 2 tbsp vegetable oil
- 1/2 onion, sliced
- 1/2 bell pepper, chopped
- 1/2 cup pineapple chunks
- 1/4 cup soy sauce
- 1/4 cup rice vinegar
- 1/4 cup ketchup
- 2 tbsp sugar
- 1/4 cup water

Instructions:

1. Dredge the pork pieces in cornstarch.
2. Heat the oil in a wok over medium-high heat. Fry the pork pieces until golden and crispy, about 5-7 minutes. Remove and set aside.
3. In the same wok, sauté the onion and bell pepper for 2-3 minutes.
4. Add the pineapple chunks, soy sauce, rice vinegar, ketchup, sugar, and water. Bring to a simmer.
5. Stir in the fried pork and coat with the sauce.
6. Serve hot with rice.

Mongolian Beef

Ingredients:

- 1 lb flank steak, thinly sliced
- 2 tbsp soy sauce
- 2 tbsp hoisin sauce
- 2 tbsp brown sugar
- 1 tbsp cornstarch
- 1/4 cup vegetable oil
- 4-5 dried red chilies
- 4 cloves garlic, minced
- 2 green onions, chopped

Instructions:

1. Toss the sliced beef with soy sauce, hoisin sauce, brown sugar, and cornstarch.
2. Heat oil in a pan or wok over medium-high heat. Add the dried chilies and garlic, cooking until fragrant.
3. Add the beef and stir-fry for 4-5 minutes until browned.
4. Stir in the green onions and cook for another 2 minutes.
5. Serve with steamed rice.

General Tso's Chicken

Ingredients:

- 1 lb chicken breast, cubed
- 1/2 cup cornstarch
- 2 tbsp soy sauce
- 2 tbsp rice vinegar
- 1 tbsp hoisin sauce
- 2 tbsp sugar
- 2 tbsp vegetable oil
- 3-4 dried chilies
- 2 cloves garlic, minced
- 1/2 tsp ginger, minced
- 2 green onions, chopped

Instructions:

1. Coat the chicken pieces in cornstarch and set aside.
2. Heat oil in a pan over medium-high heat. Fry the chicken pieces until golden brown and crispy, about 5-7 minutes. Remove and set aside.
3. In the same pan, sauté the dried chilies, garlic, and ginger.
4. Add the soy sauce, rice vinegar, hoisin sauce, and sugar. Stir to combine and bring to a simmer.
5. Add the fried chicken back into the sauce and toss to coat.
6. Garnish with green onions and serve with steamed rice.

Beef with Broccoli

Ingredients:

- 1 lb flank steak, thinly sliced
- 2 cups broccoli florets, blanched
- 2 tbsp soy sauce
- 1 tbsp oyster sauce
- 1 tbsp hoisin sauce
- 1 tbsp cornstarch
- 2 tbsp vegetable oil
- 1 clove garlic, minced
- 1/2 cup beef broth

Instructions:

1. Mix the soy sauce, oyster sauce, hoisin sauce, and cornstarch to make a marinade.
2. Marinate the beef in the sauce for 30 minutes.
3. Heat oil in a wok and stir-fry the beef until browned, about 4-5 minutes.
4. Add the garlic and cook for 1 minute.
5. Add the beef broth and broccoli, cooking until the sauce thickens.
6. Serve with steamed rice.

Sizzling Mongolian Lamb

Ingredients:

- 1 lb lamb, thinly sliced
- 2 tbsp soy sauce
- 1 tbsp hoisin sauce
- 2 tbsp brown sugar
- 1 tbsp cornstarch
- 2 tbsp vegetable oil
- 1 onion, sliced
- 2 green onions, chopped
- 1/2 tsp black pepper

Instructions:

1. In a bowl, mix soy sauce, hoisin sauce, brown sugar, and cornstarch.
2. Marinate the lamb slices in the sauce for 30 minutes.
3. Heat oil in a pan over medium-high heat. Sauté the onion and green onions until soft.
4. Add the marinated lamb and stir-fry until cooked through.
5. Sprinkle with black pepper and serve sizzling on a hot plate.

Cantonese Dim Sum

Ingredients:

- 1 package of dumpling wrappers
- 1/2 lb ground pork
- 1/4 cup shrimp, chopped
- 1/4 cup bamboo shoots, chopped
- 2 tbsp soy sauce
- 1 tbsp sesame oil
- 1/2 tsp ginger, minced
- 1/4 cup water chestnuts, chopped

Instructions:

1. In a bowl, mix the pork, shrimp, bamboo shoots, soy sauce, sesame oil, ginger, and water chestnuts.
2. Place a spoonful of filling on each dumpling wrapper.
3. Fold and seal the wrappers into small pouches.
4. Steam the dim sum in a bamboo steamer for 8-10 minutes until cooked through.
5. Serve with soy sauce and chili sauce for dipping.

Shrimp with Lobster Sauce

Ingredients:

- 1 lb shrimp, peeled and deveined
- 1/4 cup chicken broth
- 1 tbsp soy sauce
- 1 tbsp oyster sauce
- 1 tbsp cornstarch
- 2 cloves garlic, minced
- 1/4 cup fermented black beans (optional)
- 1 tbsp vegetable oil

Instructions:

1. Heat oil in a pan over medium-high heat and sauté the garlic until fragrant.
2. Add the shrimp and cook until they turn pink, about 2-3 minutes.
3. Add the chicken broth, soy sauce, oyster sauce, and black beans. Stir to combine.
4. Stir in the cornstarch to thicken the sauce and cook for 1-2 minutes.
5. Serve with steamed rice.

Hot and Sour Soup

Ingredients:

- 4 cups chicken broth
- 1/2 cup tofu, sliced into strips
- 1/4 cup wood ear mushrooms, sliced
- 1/2 cup bamboo shoots, julienned
- 1 egg, beaten
- 2 tbsp soy sauce
- 2 tbsp rice vinegar
- 1 tbsp chili paste
- 1 tsp white pepper
- 1 tbsp cornstarch
- 2 green onions, chopped

Instructions:

1. In a pot, bring chicken broth to a boil.
2. Add the tofu, wood ear mushrooms, and bamboo shoots to the broth and simmer for 5 minutes.
3. Stir in soy sauce, rice vinegar, chili paste, and white pepper.
4. Mix cornstarch with a little water and stir into the soup to thicken.
5. Slowly pour in the beaten egg while stirring the soup.
6. Garnish with green onions and serve hot.

Wonton Soup

Ingredients:

- 1/2 lb ground pork
- 1/4 lb shrimp, finely chopped
- 1 tbsp soy sauce
- 1 tsp sesame oil
- 1/2 tsp ginger, minced
- 1 clove garlic, minced
- 1 pack wonton wrappers
- 4 cups chicken broth
- 2 green onions, chopped
- 1/2 tsp white pepper

Instructions:

1. In a bowl, mix the ground pork, shrimp, soy sauce, sesame oil, ginger, and garlic.
2. Place a small amount of filling in the center of each wonton wrapper. Wet the edges with water and fold to seal.
3. Bring a pot of water to a boil. Gently drop the wontons into the water and cook for about 4-5 minutes until they float to the surface.
4. In a separate pot, bring the chicken broth to a boil. Add the cooked wontons to the broth and simmer for 2-3 minutes.
5. Garnish with chopped green onions and white pepper. Serve hot.

Egg Foo Young

Ingredients:

- 4 large eggs
- 1/2 cup cooked chicken or shrimp, chopped
- 1/4 cup mushrooms, sliced
- 1/4 cup bean sprouts
- 1/4 cup green onions, chopped
- 1/4 cup water chestnuts, chopped
- 2 tbsp soy sauce
- 1 tbsp cornstarch
- 2 tbsp vegetable oil
- 1/4 cup gravy (optional for topping)

Instructions:

1. In a bowl, whisk together eggs, soy sauce, and cornstarch.
2. Stir in chicken, mushrooms, bean sprouts, green onions, and water chestnuts.
3. Heat oil in a large skillet over medium-high heat. Pour the egg mixture into the skillet to form small pancakes.
4. Cook each pancake for 2-3 minutes per side until golden brown and cooked through.
5. Top with gravy (optional) and serve hot.

Honey Walnut Shrimp

Ingredients:

- 1 lb shrimp, peeled and deveined
- 1/4 cup mayonnaise
- 2 tbsp honey
- 1 tbsp sweetened condensed milk
- 1/4 cup walnuts, toasted
- 1/4 cup cornstarch
- Vegetable oil for frying
- 1/2 tsp sesame seeds (optional)

Instructions:

1. Toss shrimp in cornstarch to coat evenly.
2. Heat oil in a pan and fry the shrimp in batches until golden and crispy. Remove and set aside.
3. In a bowl, mix together mayonnaise, honey, and sweetened condensed milk.
4. Toss the fried shrimp in the honey sauce to coat.
5. Top with toasted walnuts and sesame seeds (optional). Serve immediately.

Braised Abalone with Shiitake Mushrooms

Ingredients:

- 4 abalone (fresh or canned)
- 1/2 lb shiitake mushrooms, sliced
- 1/4 cup soy sauce
- 1/4 cup chicken stock
- 2 tbsp sugar
- 1 tbsp sesame oil
- 1 tbsp ginger, minced
- 2 cloves garlic, minced
- 2 green onions, chopped

Instructions:

1. Heat sesame oil in a pan over medium heat. Add ginger and garlic, sautéing until fragrant.
2. Add the shiitake mushrooms and cook for 3-4 minutes until softened.
3. Pour in soy sauce, chicken stock, and sugar. Stir to combine.
4. Add the abalone and simmer for 10-15 minutes until tender.
5. Garnish with green onions and serve.

Orange Chicken

Ingredients:

- 1 lb chicken breast, cubed
- 1/4 cup cornstarch
- 1/4 cup soy sauce
- 1/4 cup orange juice
- 1/4 cup sugar
- 1/4 cup rice vinegar
- 1 tbsp ginger, minced
- 2 cloves garlic, minced
- 1/2 tsp red pepper flakes (optional)
- 2 tbsp vegetable oil

Instructions:

1. Coat the chicken pieces in cornstarch and set aside.
2. Heat oil in a pan over medium-high heat. Fry the chicken until golden and crispy, about 5-6 minutes. Remove and set aside.
3. In a bowl, mix soy sauce, orange juice, sugar, rice vinegar, ginger, garlic, and red pepper flakes.
4. Pour the sauce into the pan and simmer until it thickens, about 4-5 minutes.
5. Add the fried chicken and toss to coat. Serve with steamed rice.

Char Siu (Chinese BBQ Pork)

Ingredients:

- 2 lbs pork shoulder, cut into strips
- 1/4 cup hoisin sauce
- 1/4 cup soy sauce
- 2 tbsp honey
- 1 tbsp Chinese five-spice powder
- 2 tbsp rice wine or Shaoxing wine
- 1 tbsp sugar
- 2 cloves garlic, minced

Instructions:

1. In a bowl, mix hoisin sauce, soy sauce, honey, five-spice powder, rice wine, sugar, and garlic to make a marinade.
2. Marinate the pork in the mixture for 4-6 hours or overnight.
3. Preheat the oven to 375°F (190°C). Place the pork on a rack over a baking sheet lined with foil.
4. Roast the pork for 25-30 minutes, basting with the marinade halfway through.
5. Let the pork rest for 10 minutes before slicing. Serve with steamed rice.

Salt and Pepper Shrimp

Ingredients:

- 1 lb shrimp, peeled and deveined
- 2 tbsp cornstarch
- 1 tbsp flour
- 1/4 cup vegetable oil
- 1/4 tsp salt
- 1/4 tsp black pepper
- 2 cloves garlic, minced
- 2-3 dried red chilies (optional)
- 2 green onions, chopped

Instructions:

1. Mix cornstarch, flour, salt, and pepper in a bowl. Coat the shrimp in the mixture.
2. Heat oil in a pan over medium-high heat. Fry the shrimp in batches until golden brown and crispy.
3. Remove the shrimp and set aside. In the same pan, sauté garlic and dried chilies until fragrant.
4. Add the shrimp back into the pan and toss to coat with the garlic and chilies.
5. Garnish with chopped green onions and serve.

Chicken with Cashew Nuts

Ingredients:

- 1 lb chicken breast, sliced
- 1/4 cup cashew nuts, roasted
- 1/4 cup soy sauce
- 2 tbsp oyster sauce
- 1 tbsp rice wine
- 1 tsp sugar
- 1 tbsp cornstarch
- 2 tbsp vegetable oil
- 1/2 red bell pepper, sliced
- 2 cloves garlic, minced
- 1/2 tsp ginger, minced

Instructions:

1. In a bowl, mix soy sauce, oyster sauce, rice wine, sugar, and cornstarch to make a marinade.
2. Marinate the chicken for 15 minutes.
3. Heat oil in a pan over medium-high heat. Stir-fry the chicken until browned and cooked through.
4. Add the red bell pepper, garlic, and ginger, cooking for 2-3 minutes.
5. Stir in the cashew nuts and cook for another minute. Serve with steamed rice.

Dry-Fried Green Beans

Ingredients:

- 1 lb green beans, trimmed
- 2 tbsp vegetable oil
- 2 cloves garlic, minced
- 1/4 tsp red pepper flakes (optional)
- 1/4 cup soy sauce
- 1 tbsp sugar

Instructions:

1. Heat oil in a pan over medium-high heat. Add the green beans and stir-fry until they start to blister and turn golden brown, about 5-7 minutes.
2. Add garlic and red pepper flakes (if using) and cook for 1 more minute.
3. Stir in soy sauce and sugar, cooking for another 2 minutes until the beans are tender and coated with the sauce. Serve hot.

Lemon Chicken

Ingredients:

- 1 lb chicken breast, sliced
- 1/4 cup cornstarch
- 1/4 cup flour
- 1/4 cup soy sauce
- 2 tbsp lemon juice
- 2 tbsp honey
- 1 tbsp rice vinegar
- 1 tbsp sugar
- 1/4 tsp ginger, minced
- 2 tbsp vegetable oil
- 1/2 tsp sesame seeds (optional)

Instructions:

1. Coat the chicken pieces in cornstarch and flour.
2. Heat oil in a pan over medium-high heat and fry the chicken until golden and crispy, about 5-6 minutes.
3. In a separate bowl, mix soy sauce, lemon juice, honey, rice vinegar, sugar, and ginger to create the sauce.
4. Pour the sauce over the fried chicken and toss to coat.
5. Garnish with sesame seeds (optional) and serve with steamed rice.

Shrimp and Scallop Stir-Fry

Ingredients:

- 1/2 lb shrimp, peeled and deveined
- 1/2 lb scallops
- 2 tbsp soy sauce
- 1 tbsp rice wine
- 1 tbsp oyster sauce
- 1 tsp sugar
- 1/2 tsp cornstarch
- 1/2 cup bell peppers, sliced
- 1/2 cup snap peas
- 1/4 cup carrots, julienned
- 2 cloves garlic, minced
- 1 tbsp vegetable oil

Instructions:

1. In a bowl, mix soy sauce, rice wine, oyster sauce, sugar, and cornstarch to make a marinade.
2. Marinate the shrimp and scallops in the sauce for 15 minutes.
3. Heat oil in a wok or large pan over medium-high heat. Stir-fry the garlic until fragrant.
4. Add the bell peppers, snap peas, and carrots, and stir-fry for 2-3 minutes until they start to soften.
5. Add the shrimp and scallops, and stir-fry for 3-4 minutes until cooked through.
6. Serve hot with steamed rice.

Chinese Spicy Beef and Peppers

Ingredients:

- 1 lb beef sirloin, thinly sliced
- 2 tbsp soy sauce
- 1 tbsp hoisin sauce
- 2 tbsp rice vinegar
- 1 tbsp chili paste
- 1 tsp sugar
- 1/4 cup water
- 1 red bell pepper, sliced
- 1 green bell pepper, sliced
- 2 cloves garlic, minced
- 1 tbsp vegetable oil

Instructions:

1. In a bowl, mix soy sauce, hoisin sauce, rice vinegar, chili paste, sugar, and water to make the sauce.
2. Heat oil in a pan over medium-high heat. Stir-fry the garlic for 1 minute.
3. Add the beef and stir-fry until browned, about 4-5 minutes.
4. Add the bell peppers and cook for an additional 3-4 minutes.
5. Pour in the sauce and cook for another 2-3 minutes until the sauce thickens.
6. Serve hot with steamed rice.

Steamed Fish with Ginger and Scallions

Ingredients:

- 1 whole fish (tilapia, snapper, or bass)
- 2-inch piece of ginger, thinly sliced
- 3 green onions, chopped
- 2 tbsp soy sauce
- 1 tbsp rice wine
- 1 tsp sesame oil
- 1 tbsp vegetable oil

Instructions:

1. Clean and gut the fish, then place it on a heatproof plate.
2. Scatter the ginger slices and half of the green onions over the fish.
3. Steam the fish over high heat for 10-12 minutes, or until the fish is fully cooked.
4. In a small pan, heat the vegetable oil, soy sauce, rice wine, and sesame oil.
5. Once the fish is done, pour the hot sauce over the fish and garnish with the remaining green onions.
6. Serve immediately.

Kung Pao Shrimp

Ingredients:

- 1 lb shrimp, peeled and deveined
- 1/4 cup roasted peanuts
- 2 tbsp soy sauce
- 1 tbsp rice vinegar
- 1 tbsp hoisin sauce
- 1 tbsp chili paste
- 1 tsp sugar
- 1/2 cup bell peppers, chopped
- 1/4 cup onions, chopped
- 2 cloves garlic, minced
- 1 tbsp vegetable oil

Instructions:

1. In a bowl, mix soy sauce, rice vinegar, hoisin sauce, chili paste, and sugar to make the sauce.
2. Heat oil in a pan over medium-high heat. Stir-fry the garlic for 1 minute.
3. Add the shrimp and cook for 3-4 minutes until they turn pink.
4. Add the bell peppers, onions, and peanuts, and stir-fry for 2 minutes.
5. Pour in the sauce and cook for another 2 minutes until everything is well coated.
6. Serve hot with steamed rice.

Imperial Prawns

Ingredients:

- 1 lb large prawns, peeled and deveined
- 2 tbsp soy sauce
- 1 tbsp rice wine
- 1 tbsp oyster sauce
- 1 tbsp sugar
- 1/4 cup cornstarch
- 2 eggs, beaten
- 2 tbsp vegetable oil

Instructions:

1. In a bowl, mix soy sauce, rice wine, oyster sauce, and sugar to make a marinade.
2. Marinate the prawns for 15 minutes.
3. Coat the prawns with cornstarch, then dip them into the beaten eggs.
4. Heat oil in a pan over medium-high heat. Fry the prawns for 2-3 minutes until golden and crispy.
5. Serve immediately with a dipping sauce of your choice.

Steamed Dumplings

Ingredients:

- 1 lb ground pork or chicken
- 1/2 cup cabbage, finely chopped
- 1/4 cup green onions, chopped
- 1 tbsp ginger, minced
- 1 tbsp soy sauce
- 1 tsp sesame oil
- 1 pack dumpling wrappers
- 1 tbsp vegetable oil

Instructions:

1. In a bowl, mix ground meat, cabbage, green onions, ginger, soy sauce, and sesame oil to make the filling.
2. Place a small amount of filling in the center of each dumpling wrapper and fold to seal.
3. Steam the dumplings over high heat for 8-10 minutes, until fully cooked.
4. Serve with soy sauce or dipping sauce.

Pork and Chive Dumplings

Ingredients:

- 1 lb ground pork
- 1/2 cup chives, finely chopped
- 2 cloves garlic, minced
- 1 tbsp ginger, minced
- 1 tbsp soy sauce
- 1 tsp sesame oil
- 1 pack dumpling wrappers

Instructions:

1. In a bowl, mix ground pork, chives, garlic, ginger, soy sauce, and sesame oil to make the filling.
2. Place a small amount of filling in the center of each dumpling wrapper and fold to seal.
3. Steam or pan-fry the dumplings for 8-10 minutes or until golden and cooked through.
4. Serve with soy sauce or chili sauce.

Chinese Broccoli with Oyster Sauce

Ingredients:

- 1 bunch Chinese broccoli (gai lan)
- 2 tbsp oyster sauce
- 1 tbsp soy sauce
- 1 tsp sugar
- 1 tbsp vegetable oil

Instructions:

1. Trim the Chinese broccoli and steam it for 5-7 minutes until tender.
2. In a small bowl, mix oyster sauce, soy sauce, and sugar.
3. Heat vegetable oil in a pan and pour the sauce mixture into it, cooking for 1-2 minutes.
4. Drizzle the sauce over the steamed broccoli and serve.

Sweet and Sour Chicken

Ingredients:

- 1 lb chicken breast, cubed
- 1/4 cup cornstarch
- 1/4 cup flour
- 2 tbsp soy sauce
- 1/4 cup vinegar
- 1/4 cup ketchup
- 1/4 cup sugar
- 1/4 cup bell peppers, chopped
- 1/4 cup pineapple chunks
- 2 cloves garlic, minced
- 2 tbsp vegetable oil

Instructions:

1. Coat the chicken pieces in cornstarch and flour.
2. Heat oil in a pan and fry the chicken until golden and crispy, about 5-6 minutes. Remove and set aside.
3. In the same pan, sauté garlic for 1 minute. Add the bell peppers and pineapple chunks.
4. Mix soy sauce, vinegar, ketchup, and sugar in a bowl, and pour into the pan.
5. Add the fried chicken back into the pan and toss to coat in the sauce. Serve hot with rice.

Twice-Cooked Pork

Ingredients:

- 1 lb pork belly or pork shoulder, sliced
- 2 tbsp soy sauce
- 1 tbsp rice wine
- 1 tbsp hoisin sauce
- 1 tsp sugar
- 1 tbsp vegetable oil
- 1/2 cup leeks, chopped
- 1/2 cup bell peppers, chopped
- 2 cloves garlic, minced
- 1 tbsp ginger, minced

Instructions:

1. In a pot, boil the pork slices in water for 10 minutes. Remove and drain.
2. Heat oil in a pan and stir-fry the garlic and ginger until fragrant.
3. Add the pork slices and stir-fry until browned.
4. Add soy sauce, rice wine, hoisin sauce, and sugar, and cook for another 3-4 minutes.
5. Add leeks and bell peppers, and stir-fry for another 2-3 minutes. Serve with rice.

Eggplant with Garlic Sauce

Ingredients:

- 2 medium eggplants, cut into bite-sized pieces
- 2 tbsp soy sauce
- 1 tbsp rice vinegar
- 1 tbsp sugar
- 1 tsp cornstarch mixed with 2 tbsp water
- 2 tbsp vegetable oil
- 4 cloves garlic, minced
- 1-inch piece of ginger, minced
- 1/2 tsp chili flakes (optional)
- 2 tbsp green onions, chopped

Instructions:

1. Heat oil in a pan over medium heat. Add the eggplant and cook until browned and tender, about 8-10 minutes. Remove and set aside.
2. In the same pan, add garlic, ginger, and chili flakes (if using). Stir-fry until fragrant, about 1 minute.
3. Add soy sauce, rice vinegar, sugar, and cornstarch mixture. Stir well to combine and simmer for 2-3 minutes.
4. Return the eggplant to the pan and toss to coat with the sauce. Cook for another 2 minutes.
5. Garnish with green onions and serve.

Crispy Duck with Pancakes

Ingredients:

- 1 duck (about 4-5 lbs)
- 2 tbsp soy sauce
- 2 tbsp hoisin sauce
- 2 tbsp rice vinegar
- 1 tbsp sugar
- 1 tsp five-spice powder
- 1/4 cup vegetable oil
- 12-16 Chinese pancakes (or flour tortillas)
- 2 spring onions, sliced thinly
- 1 cucumber, julienned

Instructions:

1. Preheat the oven to 375°F (190°C). Rub the duck with soy sauce, hoisin sauce, rice vinegar, sugar, and five-spice powder.
2. Roast the duck in the oven for 1.5 to 2 hours, basting occasionally with its own juices until the skin is crispy and golden.
3. While the duck roasts, warm the pancakes by steaming them or heating them in a pan.
4. Once the duck is cooked, remove from the oven and let it rest for 10 minutes. Shred the meat, discarding the bones.
5. To serve, place a few pieces of duck, cucumber, and spring onion on a pancake. Drizzle with a little extra hoisin sauce and wrap up to eat.

Chinese Chive and Shrimp Dumplings

Ingredients:

- 1/2 lb shrimp, peeled and chopped
- 1/2 cup Chinese chives, chopped
- 1 tbsp soy sauce
- 1 tsp sesame oil
- 1/2 tsp ginger, minced
- 1/4 tsp white pepper
- 1 pack dumpling wrappers

Instructions:

1. In a bowl, combine chopped shrimp, Chinese chives, soy sauce, sesame oil, ginger, and white pepper.
2. Place a small spoonful of the filling in the center of each dumpling wrapper.
3. Fold the wrappers over the filling and seal by pleating the edges.
4. Steam the dumplings for 8-10 minutes, until cooked through.
5. Serve with soy sauce or chili oil.

Sichuan-style Chicken

Ingredients:

- 1 lb boneless chicken thighs, cut into bite-sized pieces
- 2 tbsp soy sauce
- 1 tbsp rice vinegar
- 1 tbsp hoisin sauce
- 2 tbsp chili paste or Sichuan peppercorns
- 3 cloves garlic, minced
- 1 tbsp ginger, minced
- 1/2 cup dried red chilies
- 2 tbsp vegetable oil
- 1 tbsp sugar
- 1/4 cup green onions, chopped

Instructions:

1. Heat oil in a wok over medium-high heat. Add garlic, ginger, and Sichuan peppercorns, and stir-fry until fragrant.
2. Add chicken pieces and cook until browned and cooked through, about 5-7 minutes.
3. Add dried red chilies, soy sauce, rice vinegar, hoisin sauce, sugar, and chili paste. Stir to combine.
4. Cook for an additional 3-4 minutes until the sauce thickens.
5. Garnish with green onions and serve with rice.

Beijing-style Noodles

Ingredients:

- 1 lb fresh Chinese wheat noodles (or spaghetti)
- 2 tbsp soy sauce
- 1 tbsp dark soy sauce
- 1 tbsp sesame oil
- 1/2 tbsp sugar
- 1/2 cup ground pork or beef
- 2 cloves garlic, minced
- 1 tbsp ginger, minced
- 2 green onions, chopped
- 1/2 cup cucumber, julienned (for garnish)

Instructions:

1. Cook the noodles according to the package instructions. Drain and set aside.
2. In a pan, heat sesame oil over medium-high heat. Add garlic, ginger, and ground pork or beef, and cook until browned.
3. Stir in soy sauce, dark soy sauce, and sugar. Cook for 2-3 minutes.
4. Toss the cooked noodles into the sauce and mix well to coat.
5. Garnish with green onions and cucumber. Serve immediately.

Xiao Long Bao (Soup Dumplings)

Ingredients:

- 1 lb ground pork
- 1/4 cup gelatinized pork stock (or homemade broth)
- 2 tbsp soy sauce
- 1 tbsp sesame oil
- 1 tsp sugar
- 1/2 tsp white pepper
- 1 pack dumpling wrappers

Instructions:

1. In a bowl, mix ground pork, soy sauce, sesame oil, sugar, and white pepper.
2. Heat the pork stock until it becomes a gel, then mix the gel into the pork mixture.
3. Place a small spoonful of the mixture in each dumpling wrapper and seal carefully.
4. Steam the dumplings for about 8 minutes, or until the wrapper is translucent and the filling is cooked through.
5. Serve immediately with soy sauce and vinegar.

Lotus Root with Pork Soup

Ingredients:

- 1/2 lb pork ribs
- 1 lotus root, peeled and sliced
- 2 tbsp soy sauce
- 1 tbsp rice wine
- 1/2 tsp white pepper
- 1/2 inch ginger, sliced
- 5 cups water
- 2 tbsp green onions, chopped

Instructions:

1. In a large pot, add pork ribs and water, and bring to a boil. Skim off any impurities.
2. Add soy sauce, rice wine, white pepper, ginger, and lotus root slices.
3. Simmer for 1.5 to 2 hours, until the pork is tender and the flavors are well combined.
4. Garnish with green onions and serve.

Prawns in Black Bean Sauce

Ingredients:

- 1 lb prawns, peeled and deveined
- 2 tbsp black bean paste
- 2 tbsp soy sauce
- 1 tbsp rice wine
- 1 tbsp sugar
- 2 cloves garlic, minced
- 1/2 inch ginger, minced
- 1/2 cup bell peppers, chopped
- 2 tbsp vegetable oil

Instructions:

1. Heat oil in a wok over medium-high heat. Stir-fry garlic and ginger until fragrant.
2. Add prawns and cook until they turn pink.
3. Stir in black bean paste, soy sauce, rice wine, and sugar, and cook for another 2-3 minutes.
4. Add bell peppers and stir-fry for an additional 2 minutes.
5. Serve with steamed rice.

Stir-Fried Lobster with Ginger and Scallions

Ingredients:

- 2 lobsters, shelled and cut into pieces
- 2 tbsp ginger, sliced
- 2 tbsp scallions, chopped
- 1 tbsp soy sauce
- 1 tbsp rice wine
- 1 tsp sugar
- 1 tbsp vegetable oil

Instructions:

1. Heat oil in a wok over high heat. Add ginger and stir-fry for 1 minute.
2. Add lobster pieces and stir-fry until cooked through, about 3-4 minutes.
3. Stir in soy sauce, rice wine, and sugar. Cook for another 2 minutes.
4. Garnish with scallions and serve with rice.

Shrimp Spring Rolls

Ingredients:

- 1/2 lb shrimp, peeled and cooked
- 1/2 cup lettuce, shredded
- 1/4 cup carrots, julienned
- 1/4 cup cucumber, julienned
- 12 rice paper wrappers
- 1/4 cup mint leaves
- 1/4 cup cilantro leaves
- Peanut dipping sauce

Instructions:

1. Dip each rice paper wrapper in warm water for a few seconds until soft.
2. Lay the wrapper flat, then add shrimp, lettuce, carrots, cucumber, mint, and cilantro.
3. Fold the edges of the wrapper in and roll tightly.
4. Serve with peanut dipping sauce.

Scallops with Chinese Mushrooms

Ingredients:

- 1 lb scallops
- 1/2 cup Chinese mushrooms (shiitake or oyster), sliced
- 2 tbsp soy sauce
- 1 tbsp oyster sauce
- 1 tbsp rice wine
- 1 tsp sesame oil
- 2 cloves garlic, minced
- 2 tbsp vegetable oil

Instructions:

1. Heat oil in a pan over medium-high heat. Add garlic and cook until fragrant.
2. Add scallops and cook for 2-3 minutes per side until golden.
3. Stir in mushrooms, soy sauce, oyster sauce, rice wine, and sesame oil.
4. Cook for an additional 2-3 minutes, then serve hot.

Beef Chow Fun

Ingredients:

- 1 lb beef sirloin, thinly sliced
- 1/2 lb wide rice noodles (chow fun)
- 2 tbsp soy sauce
- 1 tbsp oyster sauce
- 1 tbsp dark soy sauce
- 1 tbsp hoisin sauce
- 1/2 tsp white pepper
- 2 cloves garlic, minced
- 1/2 onion, sliced
- 1/2 bell pepper, sliced
- 1/4 cup bean sprouts
- 2 tbsp vegetable oil

Instructions:

1. Cook the rice noodles according to the package instructions. Drain and set aside.
2. Heat 1 tbsp of oil in a wok over high heat. Add the beef and stir-fry until browned. Remove and set aside.
3. In the same wok, add another tbsp of oil, then stir-fry garlic, onion, and bell pepper for 2 minutes.
4. Add the cooked rice noodles, soy sauce, oyster sauce, dark soy sauce, hoisin sauce, and white pepper. Toss to combine.
5. Add the cooked beef and bean sprouts, stir-fry for an additional 2 minutes, and serve.

Shrimp Fried Rice

Ingredients:

- 1 lb shrimp, peeled and deveined
- 3 cups cold cooked rice
- 2 eggs, beaten
- 1/2 cup peas and carrots
- 1/4 cup green onions, chopped
- 3 tbsp soy sauce
- 1 tbsp sesame oil
- 1 tbsp vegetable oil
- 1/2 tsp white pepper

Instructions:

1. Heat vegetable oil in a wok over medium-high heat. Add shrimp and cook until pink. Remove and set aside.
2. In the same wok, add sesame oil and scrambled eggs, cooking until set.
3. Add peas, carrots, green onions, and cold rice. Stir-fry for 3-4 minutes until the rice is heated through.
4. Stir in soy sauce, white pepper, and cooked shrimp. Toss to combine and serve hot.

Red-braised Pork Belly

Ingredients:

- 1 lb pork belly, cut into cubes
- 2 tbsp soy sauce
- 1 tbsp dark soy sauce
- 2 tbsp sugar
- 1 tbsp rice wine
- 2 cloves garlic, minced
- 1-inch ginger, sliced
- 2 star anise
- 2 cups water
- 2 tbsp vegetable oil
- 1 tbsp green onions, chopped

Instructions:

1. Heat oil in a pot over medium heat. Brown the pork belly pieces on all sides.
2. Add garlic, ginger, and star anise, and stir-fry until fragrant.
3. Stir in soy sauce, dark soy sauce, sugar, and rice wine. Add water and bring to a boil.
4. Reduce heat and simmer for 1-1.5 hours until the sauce thickens and the pork is tender.
5. Garnish with chopped green onions and serve with steamed rice.

Cantonese Roast Chicken

Ingredients:

- 1 whole chicken (about 3 lbs)
- 2 tbsp soy sauce
- 1 tbsp hoisin sauce
- 1 tbsp rice wine
- 1 tbsp honey
- 1/2 tsp five-spice powder
- 1 tbsp sesame oil
- 3 cloves garlic, minced
- 2-inch piece of ginger, sliced
- 1/4 cup green onions, chopped

Instructions:

1. Preheat the oven to 375°F (190°C). Rub the chicken with soy sauce, hoisin sauce, rice wine, honey, five-spice powder, sesame oil, garlic, and ginger.
2. Roast the chicken for 1.5 hours, basting every 30 minutes, until the skin is golden brown and the chicken is cooked through.
3. Let the chicken rest for 10 minutes before carving. Garnish with chopped green onions.

Fried Tofu with Vegetables

Ingredients:

- 1 block firm tofu, cut into cubes
- 1/2 cup mushrooms, sliced
- 1/2 cup bell peppers, sliced
- 1/2 cup zucchini, sliced
- 2 tbsp soy sauce
- 1 tbsp sesame oil
- 1 tbsp hoisin sauce
- 1 tbsp rice vinegar
- 1/4 cup green onions, chopped
- 1/4 tsp white pepper
- Vegetable oil for frying

Instructions:

1. Heat oil in a pan over medium heat. Fry the tofu cubes until golden and crispy on all sides. Remove and set aside.
2. In the same pan, add sesame oil, mushrooms, bell peppers, and zucchini. Stir-fry for 3-4 minutes.
3. Add soy sauce, hoisin sauce, rice vinegar, white pepper, and cooked tofu. Toss to coat.
4. Garnish with green onions and serve with rice.

Stir-fried Asparagus with Shrimp

Ingredients:

- 1 lb shrimp, peeled and deveined
- 1 bunch asparagus, cut into 2-inch pieces
- 2 cloves garlic, minced
- 1 tbsp soy sauce
- 1 tbsp rice wine
- 1 tbsp sesame oil
- 1 tbsp vegetable oil
- 1/4 tsp white pepper
- 2 tbsp green onions, chopped

Instructions:

1. Heat vegetable oil in a wok over medium-high heat. Stir-fry shrimp until pink and cooked through. Remove and set aside.
2. In the same wok, add sesame oil and garlic. Stir-fry for 30 seconds.
3. Add asparagus and stir-fry for 3-4 minutes until tender.
4. Stir in soy sauce, rice wine, white pepper, and shrimp. Toss to combine.
5. Garnish with green onions and serve.

Crab Rangoon

Ingredients:

- 8 oz cream cheese, softened
- 1/2 cup crab meat, chopped
- 2 tbsp green onions, chopped
- 1 tsp soy sauce
- 1/2 tsp garlic powder
- 1 pack wonton wrappers
- Vegetable oil for frying

Instructions:

1. In a bowl, mix cream cheese, crab meat, green onions, soy sauce, and garlic powder.
2. Place a spoonful of the filling in the center of each wonton wrapper. Moisten the edges with water and fold to seal.
3. Heat oil in a pan over medium heat. Fry the crab rangoon until golden brown, about 3-4 minutes.
4. Drain on paper towels and serve with sweet and sour sauce.

Hot Pot with Tofu and Vegetables

Ingredients:

- 1 block tofu, cut into cubes
- 1/2 cup mushrooms, sliced
- 1/2 cup bok choy, chopped
- 1/2 cup napa cabbage, chopped
- 2 cups vegetable broth
- 2 tbsp soy sauce
- 1 tbsp sesame oil
- 2 cloves garlic, minced
- 1-inch ginger, sliced
- 2 tbsp green onions, chopped
- 1/2 tsp chili flakes (optional)

Instructions:

1. In a hot pot or large pot, heat sesame oil over medium heat. Add garlic and ginger, and stir-fry for 1 minute.
2. Add vegetable broth, soy sauce, and chili flakes (if using). Bring to a boil.
3. Add tofu, mushrooms, bok choy, and napa cabbage. Simmer for 5-7 minutes until the vegetables are tender.
4. Garnish with green onions and serve with rice.